MW01106702

CAST IRON SIGNS

OF

PENNSYLVANIA TOWNS

AND OTHER LANDMARKS

N. CLAIR CLAWSER

SUNBURY PRESS

Mechanicsburg, PA USA

Published by Sunbury Press, Inc.
105 South Market Street
Mechanicsburg, Pennsylvania 17055

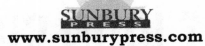

www.sunburypress.com

For information about special discounts for bulk purchases, please contact Sunbury Press Orders Dept. at (855) 338-8359 or orders@sunburypress.com.

To request one of our authors for speaking engagements or book signings, please contact Sunbury Press Publicity Dept. at publicity@sunburypress.com.

ISBN: 978-1-62006-737-6 (Hard cover)

Library of Congress Number: 2016944605

FIRST SUNBURY PRESS EDITION: July 2016

Product of the United States of America
0   1   1   2   3   5   8   13   21   34   55

Set in Bookman Old Style
Designed by Crystal Devine
Cover by Lawrence Knorr
Edited by Lawrence Knorr

Continue the Enlightenment!

Contents

Foreword

Have you taken notice of those cast iron signs that are located throughout the Commonwealth of Pennsylvania?

I first did back in 1960 at the age of 15. The germ of an idea planted back then has grown into this informative book. A family tree of interest.

Pennsylvania is unique with this type of town sign, which could become a thing of the past. (New York State has many cast iron signs, too, but they are on many subjects and not necessarily on town names.) Almost from the start I noticed some of these signs were being removed, even as I discovered that many still remained. Originally cast from about 1929 until 1942, these signs were made largely in either the Carlisle Foundry in Carlisle or Geiser Manufacturing Company in Waynesboro. Both companies are long out of business. There are a small number that were produced elsewhere, but not many. (Allegheny Foundry.)

Jack Graham of the Keystone Markers Trust stated that the Department of Highways report for 1928-1930 said, "During the biennium 1,359 information signs were placed including historical, stream, state institution, speed limit and parking restriction signs."

Many of these signs endure to this day, but are in constant danger of removal. A few new ones have been posted, but many more should be. The afore-mentioned report does not say how many were town signs. If the total was all towns and divided by 4 that would only be 339 towns. There are numerous stream signs still in existence today. These are 2 sided with just the name. Town signs are one-sided. We can only imagine that each town that had a cast iron sign may have had 4, one for each direction. Very few towns, that still have a sign, have more than two today. Hanover, a rarity, has six. Gettysburg has 4, as does Jonestown. York New Salem has 3, as does Lemoyne. Rothsville had 4, but one was removed. Schoeneck has 4 new ones installed by the Keystone Markers Trust, and Mountville has 3.

While being a pioneer in preserving these signs, I am not alone. My brother Bill has supplied me with much help, taking pictures, and accompanying me on numerous sign-hunting trips. His interest in ghost towns led me to delve into this subject more than before.

Along the line, Robert P. Walsh has been a large help in spotting town signs that I had not discovered before and Michael G. Visali sparked the interest in taking pictures of these signs. Members of the Keystone Markers Trust also provided information and showed much interest: John T. "Jack" Graham (also known as "Pennsylvania Jack") a retired Pennsylvania State Park Manager, has repaired numerous signs and got them reposted; Nathan Guest is President of the Trust; Jim Carn has repainted over 50 signs, accompanied by his faithful dog; Michael Wintermantel has repainted a number of signs in western Pennsylvania, too.

I get information here and there of individuals who have had a part in repairing or repainting a sign. The list is growing:

Elaine Bowman	Giovina Bradley
Jim Carn	Bruce Clark
N. Clair Clawser (Yours Trully)	Bill Clawser
Ted & Janet Clouse	Francis Ditzler
Freda Fasnacht	John T. "Jack" Graham
Nathan Guest	Duane McClain
Karen, Melissa, & Erica Kreiger	Don Roades, Jr.
Victor Schall	Russell E. Snyder
Terry Stump	Michael G. Visali
Robert P. Walsh	Michael Wintermantel
Fred Yenerall	

One of the largest causes of signs disappearing has been being hit by a car or a snow plow. A few people have come forward and helped to get a sign replaced. Then too, the Highway Department has removed signs when a road gets widened or improved. Without public interest and action, these signs could become an icon of the past.

We do not claim the list of pictures in this book to be totally complete, but is the author's total collection. Unfortunately, I did not take pictures the first few years of this study, I only wrote down the information on the signs. By the time I started to take pictures, many signs had disappeared. Some towns claim to have had a sign, which we have not been able to document by obtaining a real picture. Beware of the computer-generated pictures that can be produced today. They are not a genuine representation of these signs.

Cameras were so limiting before the digital camera, so I did not take pictures very often at first. Remember, film had only 12 or 24 pictures per roll. I did take numerous pictures before my unfortunate house fire in 1999, which damaged most of the pictures to some degree. After 1999, I attempted to retake all of the town signs but found many were not posted anymore, and therefore the damaged pictures were the only ones available. With the advent of the digital camera, I retook over the rest of remaining signs again. The damaged photos in this book are marked with an asterisk (*).

Through personal contact and the help of others we have made up this list of photos. Some of the pictures in this compilation are of signs that are not up anymore, and their whereabouts are unknown. (Marysville, Middleburg, Hinkletown, Johnstown, etc.) Some signs we saw but did not document in time are: Sylvania, McAdoo, Altoona, etc.

I have marveled for years that Pennsylvania, a state that ranks as the 33rd in size among the 50 states has been in the top 3 and now 6 states in population. (There are only 8 states that have over 10 million people.) The Keystone State has been very industrious and productive in many categories, and while full of many attractions, still has great forests. The State with the largest rural population, it has great hunting and fishing locations. Today, it has become a great State for the Senior Citizens with many retirement communities.

Pennsylvania has 67 counties, as does Alabama, Florida and South Dakota. Nineteen states have more than 67 counties, with Texas having the most (254) and Delaware the least (3).

I hope this book will help you enjoy the Keystone State more than before.

N. Clair Clawser

Who is Neb Nilknarf? See author page for the answer.

ADAMS COUNTY

Named for John Adams, who was the U.S. President at the time it was formed. Formed in 1800. Area – 526 sq. mi. Area rank – 44th. County Seat: Gettysburg.

ABBOTTSTOWN - Planned and named for John Abbott. Founded 1756.

ARENDTSVILLE - Named for John Arendt. Founded 1808.

BENDERSVILLE - Named for Henry Bender - pioneer. Founded 1832.

BIGLERVILLE - Named for Gov. William Bigler. Founded 1817.

CASHTOWN - Name derived from a remark made to tavern keeper who demanded cash payment. Founded 1800.

EAST BERLIN - Named for Berlin, Germany. Founded 1764.

FAIRFIELD - Named for Fairfield, England. Founded 1801.

GETTYSBURG - Named for James Gettys, one of the first settlers. Founded 1780.

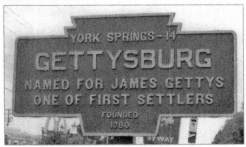

HEIDLERSBURG - Originally Starrytown. Renamed for John Heidler. Founded 1812.

LITTLESTOWN - Named for Peter Little. Founded 1765.

McKNIGHTSTOWN- Originally New Salem, renamed for Thomas McKnight. Founded 1845.

McSHERRYSTOWN - Planned by and named for Patrick Mc-Sherry. Founded 1783.

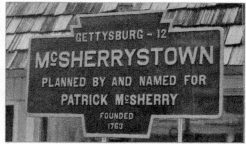

NEW OXFORD - From ox-head sign of old inn and ford near town. Founded 1792.

YORK SPRINGS - Named for local sulphur springs. Founded 1800.

ALLEGHENY COUNTY

Name origin uncertain, possible tribal name Allegewi, identified with Talligeqi, "People of the cave country." Formed in 1787. Area – 728 sq. mi. Area rank – 30th. County seat: Pittsburgh.

BOSTON - Named for Boston, Massachusetts. Founded 1886.

BRACKENRIDGE - Named for Judge Hugh H. Brackenridge.

CASTLE SHANNON - Named for early settlers home in which they lived. Founded 1879.

CHURCHILL - Incorporated 1934. Named for Beulah Church, on hill where General Forbes camped in 1758.

CLINTON - Named for famous Fox Hound Clinton. Founded 1800.

CRAFTON BORO - Named after Charles C. Craft. Founded 1830.

EAST McKEESPORT - The east end of McKeesport after McKee family pioneers.

ELIZABETH BOROUGH - Named by Colonel Stephen Bayard for his wife Elizabeth. Founded 1834.

FOREST HILLS - Named because of its similarity to Forest Hills, Long Island, New York. Founded 1919.

INGRAM - Welcome to Ingram. Ingram Board of Trade.

McKEES ROCKS - Named for early pioneer settlers of that name. Founded 1786.

VERSAILLES BORO - Formerly part of Versailles Township. Named for Versailles, France. Founded 1890.

WARRENDALE - Named for Warren Family. Formerly "Brush Creek." Founded 1907.

WEXFORD - Named for city in Ireland. Founded 1800.

ARMSTRONG COUNTY

Named for General John Armstrong. Formed in 1800.
Area – 652 sq. mi. Area rank – 34th tie.
County Seat: Kittanning.

COWANSVILLE - Named for John Cowan, pioneer settler. Founded 1849.

ELDERTON - Formerly New Middleton, named for Sara Elder. Founded 1822.

KITTANNING - From the Indian word Kit-Hanne-Ing meaning "The place at the great river." Founded 1727.

LEECHBURG - Named for David Leech, early settler and hunter. Founded 1832.

PARKER - Named for John Parker. Founded 1786.

WEST KITTANNING - Formerly Bellville. Founded by John Cunningham, early settler.

BEAVER COUNTY

**Named for Big Beaver River or Creek. Formed in 1800.
Area – 440 sq. mi. Area rank – 51st.
County Seat: Beaver.**

AMBRIDGE - Formerly Economy, renamed for American Bridge Company. Founded 1795.

BEAVER - Named for King Beaver, Lenni-Lenape Indian chief. Founded 1778.

DARLINGTON - Formerly "Greensburg" renamed for Samuel P. Darlington. Founded 1794.

FAIRVIEW - Named for its fine prospect.

FALLSTON - Meaning "A town by the falls." Founded 1799.

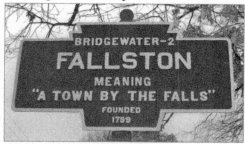

FRANKFORD SPRINGS - Named for Frankford near Philadelphia. Founded 1772.*

HOMEWOOD - Named by James Wood, early settler. Founded 1859.

HOOKSTOWN - Named for Hook pioneer family. Founded 1797.

INDUSTRY - Named for early coal and lumber industries. Founded 1836.

KOPPEL - Named for Arthur Koppel, noted manufacturer. Founded 1912.

NEW BRIGHTON - Named for Brighton, England. Founded 1786.

NEW GALILEE - Biblical name. Founded 1854.

OHIOVILLE - Named because of nearness to Ohio River. Founded 1805.

VANPORT - Named for President Martin Van Buren. Founded 1835.

BEDFORD COUNTY

**Named for town and township of Bedford, which was
named for the English Duke of Bedford. Formed in
1771. Area – 1018 sq. mi. Area rank – 9th.
County Seat: Bedford.**

NEW PARIS - Named for Capitol city of France. Founded 1846.

PLEASANTVILLE - Formerly called Dubbstown. Incorporated
   1871.*

RAINSBURG - Named for pioneer hunter John Rains. Founded
   1800.
ST. CLAIRSVILLE - Named for General Arthur St. Clair. Founded 1820.

SAXTON - Named for James Saxton. Founded 1854.

WOODBURY - Named for Woodbury, England. Founded 1800.

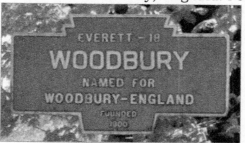

BERKS COUNTY

**Named for Berkshire, England, where the Penn family
held large estates. Formed in 1752. Area – 862 sq. mi.
Area rank – 18th. County Seat: Reading.**

BAUMSTOWN - Named for Dr. John Christian Baum. Founded
1800.

BERNVILLE - Named by earliest settlers for Berne, Switzerland.
Founded 1819. Incorporated 1851.

BETHEL - Formerly "Millersburg," named for Michael Miller, pioneer landowner. Founded 1814.

BIRDSBORO - Named for William Bird, first settler. Founded 1740.

BOYERTOWN - Named for an early settler, Henry Boyer. Founded 1835.

GOUGLERSVILLE - Named for Philip Gougler. Founded 1855.*

HAMBURG - Named for Hamburg, Germany. Founded 1772.

LENHARTSVILLE - Named for Lenhart family, first settlers. Founded 1842.

MAXATAWNY - From the Indian name, Maxatawny. Founded 1830.

MOHRSVILLE - Named for the first settlers, the Mohr family. Founded 1836.

MONTEREY - Named for the town of Monterey in Mexico. Founded 1847.

MORGANTOWN - Laid out by Jacob Morgan, Revolutionary patriot. Founded 1770.

MT. AETNA - Formerly "Wohleberstown," named for Peter Wohleber, pioneer. Founded 1810.

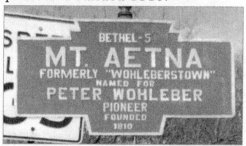

NEW SCHAEFFERSTOWN - Named for John Schaeffer, pioneer settler. Founded 1836.

ROBESONIA - Named for early settler, Henry P. Robeson. Founded 1855.

SEYFERT - Named for Seyfert Rolling Mills. Founded 1880.

SHARTLESVILLE - Named for Colonel Peter Shartle, pioneer settler and soldier. Founded 1765.

SHILLINGTON - Named for Samuel Schilling. Founded 1865.
SHOEMAKERSVILLE - Named for early settlers, Henry and Charles Shoemaker. Founded 1765.

SINKING SPRING - Named for a periodical spring on its eastern border. Founded 1793.

STONY CREEK MILLS - Named for nearby mountain stream. Founded 1879.

STOUCHSBURG - Named for one of first settlers, Andrew Stouch. Founded 1832.

STRAUSSTOWN - Named for John Strauss, who laid out town. Founded 1840.

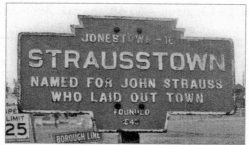

WERNERSVILLE - Named for William Werner, who laid out the town. Founded 1854.

WOMELSDORF - Named for John Womelsdorf, early settler. Founded 1782.

WYOMISSING - Named for creek on its southern border. Founded 1906.

BLAIR COUNTY

**Named for John Blair. The only county in the State
named for a purely local celebrity. Formed in 1846.
Area – 530 sq. mi. Area rank – 43rd.
County Seat: Hollidaysburg.**

ROARING SPRING - Named from sound produced by waterfall of spring near town. Founded 1865.

BRADFORD COUNTY

**Named for William Bradford, second Attorney General
of the United States, and great-grandson of William
Bradford, the first printer in Philadelphia.
Formed in 1810. Area – 1148 sq. mi. Area rank – 2nd.
County Seat: Towanda.**

ALBA - Named for cathedral town in Italy. Founded 1803.*

ATHENS - Originally "Tioga Point," renamed from Athens, Greece. Founded 1773.

BURLINGTON - Named after Burlington, Vermont. Founded 1790.

CAMPTOWN - Named for Job Camp, pioneer hunter and settler. Founded 1793.

DURELL - Named for Stephan Durell, Huguenot pioneer.
GILLETT - Named for Deacon Asa Gillett, pioneer settler. Founded 1783.*

LERAYSVILLE - Named for LeRay DeChamont. Founded 1798.

MONROETON - Named for President James Monroe. Founded
   1796.

NEW ALBANY - Named for Fort Aibany, now Albany, N.Y.
   Founded 1805.
ROME - Named for "The Eternal City." Founded 1795.

SAYRE - Named for Robert Sayre, financier. Founded 1870.

TOWANDA - From the Indian. Here our great dead are resting."
Founded 1784.

WYSOX - From the Indian, Wisachgimi, meaning a Place of Grapes. Founded 1773.

BUCKS COUNTY

Abbreviated from Buckinghamshire. Formed in 1682.
One of the three original counties of the State.
Area – 614 sq. mi. Area rank – 36th.
County Seat: Doylestown.

LAHASKA - An Indian name first applied to a nearby stream. Founded 1725.

NEW BRITAIN - Named for New Britain Township. Founded 1850.

NEW HOPE - Originally Well's Ferry, renamed New Hope in 1800. Founded 1719.

NEWTOWN - Named by William Penn. County Seat of Bucks County for 88 years. Founded 1683.

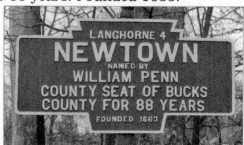

OTTSVILLE - Formerly Red Hill, renamed for Ott family. Founded 1768.

PERKASIE - Named for Manor of Perkasie, a land grant of the time of William Penn. Founded 1870.

PLEASANT VALLEY - Name suggested by location. Founded 1767.

RICHLANDTOWN - Named for Richland Township. Founded 1804.

SELLERSVILLE - Named after Samuel Sellers, early settler. Founded 1738. Incorporated 1874.

SOUTHAMPTON - Named for township and town in England. Founded 1720.

YARDLEY - Settled by Yardley family, site of Yardley's Ferry and Mill. Founded 1682.

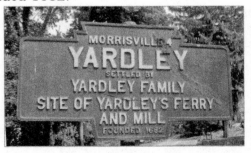

BUTLER COUNTY

Named for General Richard Butler. Formed in 1800.
Area – 794 sq. ml. Area rank – 25th.
County Seat: Butler.

BUTLER - Named after General Richard Butler. Founded 1797.*

MARS - Named after the star of Mars. Founded 1876.

SAXONBURG - Welcomes you. John A. Roebling founder. 1832. Inventor of wire rope.

CAMBRIA COUNTY

Named for Cambria Township. Formed in 1804.
Area – 692 sq. mi. Area rank – 31st.
County Seat: Ebensburg.

ASHVILLE - Named for old Ashland Iron Furnace. Founded 1887.
BELSANO - Named for town in Italy.
CHEST SPRINGS - Named for two famous springs in Chest Manor. Founded 1858.

CRESSON - Named for John Cresson, early financier. Founded 1855.

JOHNSTOWN - Named for Joseph Johns, founder. Founded 1869.

LILLY - Named for founder, Richard Lilly. Founded 1807.
LORETTO - Named for Loretto, Italy. Founded 1801.
MUNDY'S CORNER - Named for Mundy family of pioneers. Founded 1921.

NANTY GLO - From the Welsh, "Streams of coal." Founded 1810.

SPANGLER - Named for Colonel Jackson Spangler. Founded 1893.

SUMMERHILL - Originally Somerhill, named for Joseph and David Somers. Founded 1810.

WILMORE - Named by Bernard Wilmore. Founded 1931.

CAMERON COUNTY

Named for Simon Cameron, former United States Senator. (For 18 years.) He was long the "Czar of Pennsylvania Politics," Formed in 1860. Area – 401 sq. mi. Area rank – 56th. County Seat: Emporium.

CARBON COUNTY

Named for Anthracite coal deposits. Formed in 1843. Area – 404 sq. mi. Area rank – 55th. County Seat: Jim Thorpe.

CENTRE COUNTY

Geographic center of the Commonwealth. Formed in 1800. Area – 1115 sq. mi. Area rank – 5th. County Seat: Bellefonte.

AARONSBURG - Founded by Aaron Levy in 1786. Home of St. Peter's United Church of Christ = 1790.

BELLEFONTE - From the French for "Beautiful Fountain." Founded 1769.

MONUMENT - Named for Monument Rock. Huge rock in middle of stream, a landmark of Indian days. Founded 1903.

ORVISTON - Named for Judge Ellis S. Orvis. Founded 1904.

PORT MATILDA - Named in honor of the daughter of Clem Beck-with. Founded 1842.

WOODWARD - Settled by John Motz in 1768. Home of - 1806 Trinity UN. Meth. Church - 1957. Woodward Inn - 1814. P.O.S. of A. - 1893.

CHESTER COUNTY

Named for Cheshire, England. Formed in 1682. (One of the three original counties in State.) Area – 761 sq. mi. Area rank – 27th. County Seat: West Chester.

ATGLEN - Named from its location in North Valley.

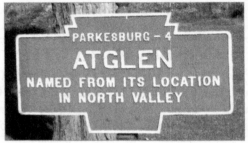

AVONDALE - Named for River Avon in England. Founded 1893.

BERWYN - Formerly Reeseville, renamed from Welsh Mountains. Founded 1878.

COCHRANVILLE - Formerly "Cochran's Inn." Named for James Cochran, early settler. Founded 1725.

DOWNINGTOWN - Formerly Milltown, renamed for Thomas Downing. Founded 1716.

HONEY BROOK - Formerly Waynesburg, named for General Anthony Wayne. Founded 1712.

KENNETT SQUARE - Named for River Kennett, England. Founded 1740.

KIMBERTON - Named for Emmor Kimber, founder of the Kimber Boarding School, May 1, 1818.

LENAPE - Named for the Lennie-Lenape or Delaware Indians.

OXFORD - Named for Oxford, England. Founded 1801.

PAOLI - Named for the Corsican General, Paoli. Founded 1755.

PARKESBURG - Named for Parke family, pioneer landowners. Founded 1872.

PHOENIXVILLE - Named for fabulous bird that rose out of fire into new life. Founded 1849.

SADSBURYVILLE - Named for Sudbury, England. Settled 1729.

SPRING CITY - Formerly Springville. Name derived from existence of numerous springs. Founded 1850.

WEST CHESTER - Originally Turk's Head, renamed for Chester. Founded 1788.

WEST GROVE - Name due to location west of London Grove Meeting. Founded 1893.

CLARION COUNTY
Named for Clarion River. Formed in 1839.
Area – 597 sq. mi. Area rank – 38th.
County Seat: Clarion.

CLARION - Named for Clarion River. Founded 1840.

CLEARFIELD COUNTY
Named for Clearfield Creek. Formed in 1804.
Area – 1139 sq. mi. Area rank – 4th.
County Seat: Clearfield.

KARTHAUS - Named for Peter A. Karthaus, pioneer landowner. Founded 1841.

WESTOVER - Named for three brothers, William, Joseph and Jonathan Westover. Founded 1840.

WOODLAND - Named for its immense timber wealth.

CLINTON COUNTY

Probably named for DeWitt Clinton, a former Governor of New York. Formed in 1839. Area – 899 sq. mi. Area rank – 15th. County Seat: Lock Haven.

COLUMBIA COUNTY

Poetic name for America, derived from Columbus, a name popularized by Joseph Hopkinson's song "Hail Columbia." Formed in 1813. Area – 484 sq. mi. Area rank – 47th. County Seat: Bloomsburg.

ALMEDIA - From the Spanish word alamedia meaning "Land of Gardens." Founded 1852.

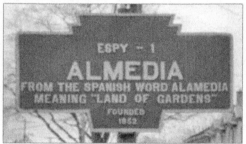

BRIAR CREEK - Named after the stream, Briar Creek. Founded 1793.

CATAWISSA - Named for Catawissa Indian tribe. Founded 1774.

ESPY - Founded by John Espy. Founded 1814.

LIME RIDGE - Named for ridge of limestone. Formerly Centreville. Founded 1845.

MAINVILLE - Name selected to indicate most important village in Main Township. Founded 1800.

MILLVILLE - Named for grist mill erected on site of town. Founded 1772.*

ORANGEVILLE - Named by first settlers, emigrants from Orange Co., N.J., for that county. Founded 1780.

RUPERT - Named for Rupert family of pioneers. Founded 1788.

CRAWFORD COUNTY

Named for Colonel William Crawford. Formed in 1800.
Area – 1012. sq. mi. Area rank – 10th.
County Seat: Meadville.

CENTERVILLE - Named for location of tract of land. Founded 1795.

CONNEAUT LAKE - From the Indian, "snow waters." Founded 1798.

HYDETOWN - Named for Elijah Hyde. Founded 1796.

MEADVILLE - Home of Allegheny College. Founded 1815.

SAEGERTOWN - Named Saeger's Mill by first settlers. Founded 1796.

TITUSVILLE - Founded by Jonathan Titus in 1796. Home of Drake Well. Birthplace of the oil industry.

VENANGO - The earlier Indian name for French Creek. Founded 1797.

CUMBERLAND COUNTY

**Named for Cumberland County, England. Formed in
1750. Area – 555 sq. mi. Area rank – 40th.
County Seat: Carlisle.**

CAMP HILL - Named from adjoining camp ground. Founded
1756.

CARLISLE - Named for Carlisle, England. Founded 1751.

CENTERVILLE - Named from location midway between Carlisle
and Shippensburg. Founded 1802.
HOGESTOWN - Named for John Hogue. Founded 1820.

LEMOYNE - Formerly named Bridgeport. Incorporated 1906.

MECHANICSBURG - Named for settlement of mechanics. Founded 1820.

MT. HOLLY SPRINGS - From Holly tree in mountain gap near town. Founded 1785.

NEWBURG - Named for Newburg, Germany. Founded 1826.

NEW CUMBERLAND - Formerly Haldemanstown. Named for Cumberland, England. Founded 1814.

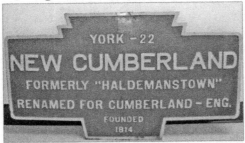

NEW KINGSTOWN - Named for John King. Founded 1818.
NEWVILLE - Meaning New Village. Founded 1794.

SHEPHERDSTOWN - Named for William Shepherd. Founded 1822.

SHIREMANSTOWN - Named for Samuel Shireman. Founded 1874.

WALNUT BOTTOM - Named for grove of walnut trees. Founded 1819.

WORMLEYSBURG - Named for John Wormley. Founded 1815.

DAUPHIN COUNTY

Named for the hereditary title of the eldest son of a French King. Formed in 1785. Area – 518 sq. mi. Area rank – 45th. County Seat: Harrisburg.

BERRYSBURG - Named from "Berry's Mountain." Founded 1819.

DAUPHIN - Formerly Green's Mill, renamed for a Dauphin of France. Founded 1770.

ELIZABETHVILLE - Originally called "Benderstettle." Founded 1817.

GRATZ - Named for Simon Gratz. Founded 1805.

HARRISBURG - Formerly Harris' Ferry, renamed for the first settler. Founded 1732.

HERSHEY - Named for M. S. Hershey. Founded 1903.

HUMMELSTOWN - Originally called Fredericktown for founder Frederick Hummel. Founded 1761.

LINGLESTOWN - Formerly the town of St. Thomas, named for Thomas Lingle. Founded 1765.

LYKENS - Originally called Lykenstown for John Lykens. Founded 1826.

MIDDLETOWN - Named from location between Lancaster and Carlisle. Founded 1720.*

MILLERSBURG - Named for Daniel Miller, founder. Founded 1807.

PENBROOK - Formerly East Harrisburg. Founded 1894.

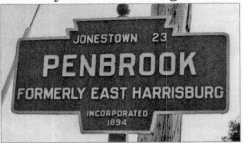

WICONISCO - From the Indian name meaning, "A wet and muddy camp." Founded 1839.

WILLIAMSTOWN - From Williams Valley in which town is located. Founded 1826.

DELAWARE COUNTY

Named for the Delaware River. Formed in 1789.
Area – 184 sq. mi. Area rank – 65th.
County Seat: Media.

BROOMALL - Named in 1868 for the Honorable John M. Broomall. Founded 1798.

CHESTER - Formerly Upland, renamed in 1682 by William Penn. Founded 1682.

CLIFTON HEIGHTS - Named after residence of Henry Lewis, a Welsh Quaker. Founded 1895.

EAST LANSDOWNE - Formerly Pembrooke and Fernwood. Incorporated as East Lansdowne in 1911. Founded 1902.

GLENOLDEN - Named for Olden family and Glen for surrounding shady nook. Founded 1894.

LANSDOWNE - Named for Lord Lansdowne's estate in England. Founded 1893.

NORWOOD - Named after novel called "Norwood." Incorporated 1893.

RIDLEY PARK - Named for a village in Cheshire, England. Incorporated 1857.

RIDLEY TOWNSHIP - First settled circa 1643. Established 1687, William Penn landgrant to John Simcock. Incorporated 1906.

RUTLEDGE - Named for Ann Rutledge, early sweetheart of Abraham Lincoln. Founded 1886.

SHARON HILL - Named for Sharon School. Incorporated 1890.

WAYNE - Formerly Louella, renamed for General Anthony Wayne. Founded 1880.

YEADON - Entering Yeadon Borough.

ELK COUNTY

**Named for Elk Creek, or the presence of elks. Formed
in 1843. Area – 807 sq. mi. Area rank – 23rd.
County Seat: Ridgway.**

BROCKPORT - Settled by Nicholas Brockway, pioneer landowner. Founded 1847.

ERIE COUNTY

**Named for Lake Erie. Formed in 1800.
Area – 813 sq. mi. Area rank – 22nd.
County Seat: Erie.**

UNION CITY - "A union of the cities." Founded 1800.

FAYETTE COUNTY

**Named for Roche Yves Gilbert Motier, Marquis de la
Fayette. Formed in 1783. Area – 802 sq. mi. Area
rank – 24th. County Seat: Uniontown.**

CONNELLSVILLE - Named for Zachariah Connell, pioneer.
Founded 1773.
FARMINGTON - Named for the farming country surrounding
the town. Founded 1841.
NEW SALEM - Named for Salem, Massachusetts. Founded
1799.
OHIOPYLE - Formerly Falls City, renamed from the Greek
"Ohiophella." Founded 1868.

UNIONTOWN - Named from union of several small villages. Founded 1776.

FOREST COUNTY

Named for its many forests within its boundary.
Formed in 1848. Area – 419 sq. mi. Area rank – 54th.
County Seat: Tionesta.
(The county with the smallest population in State.)

FRANKLIN COUNTY

Named for Benjamin Franklin. Formed in 1784.
Area – 754 sq. mi. Area rank – 28th.
County Seat: Chambersburg.

CHAMBERSBURG - Named for Colonel Benjamin Chambers. Founded 1734.

FANNETTSBURG - Founded 1793.
FORT LOUDON - Named after Ft. Loudon, a frontier fort built in 1756. Founded 1804.*

GREENCASTLE - Named for Greencastle in the north of Ireland. Founded 1750.

GREEN VILLAGE - Named for Major General Greene of the Revolutionary Army. Founded 1748.

MARION - Named for General Marion, a Revolutionary General. Founded 1748.

MERCERSBURG - Named for General Hugh Mercer. Founded 1750.

ORRSTOWN - Named for John and William Orr. Founded 1838.

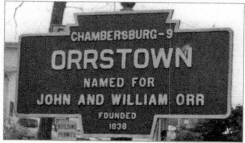

ROXBURY - Named for town in England. Founded 1778.

ST. THOMAS - Named for General Thomas Campbell. Founded 1737.*

SHADY GROVE - Named for location in virgin forest. Founded 1840.

SPRING RUN - Named for a nearby mountain stream. Founded 1764.

STATE LINE - Named thus because it is on state line. Founded 1812.

STOUFFERSTOWN - Named for Daniel Stouffer who built a mill here in 1792. Founded 1773.

WAYNESBORO - Named for General Anthony Wayne. Founded 1749.

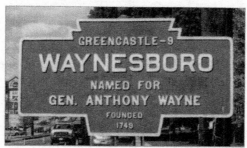

FULTON COUNTY

**Named for Robert Fulton. (Of steamboat fame.) Formed
in 1850. Area – 435 sq. mi. Area rank – 52nd.
County Seat: McConnellsburg.**

BURNT CABINS - To pacify Indians cabins of intruding white
settlers burned here 1750 by order of the provincial
government.

HUSTONTOWN - Named after early settler Thomas Huston.
Founded 1835.

McCONNELLSBURG - Named for first settlers Daniel and William McConnell. Founded 1786.

GREENE COUNTY

**Named for General Nathaniel Greene. (Most SW County
of State.) Formed in 1796. Area – 578 sq. mi.
Area rank – 39th. County Seat: Waynesburg.**

GREENSBORO - Named for Nathaniel Greene. Founded 1781.

NEW FREEPORT - Free port of trading, founded by W. P. Hoskin-
son. Founded 1849. (Most SW sign of this type in State.)

NINEVEH - Named for old city in Near East. Founded 1845.

ROGERSVILLE - Named for John Rodgers, early settler. Founded 1807.

WAYNESBURG - Named for General "Mad Anthony" Wayne. Founded 1789.

WIND RIDGE - Named because of high elevation. Founded 1792.

HUNTINGDON COUNTY

Named for the town of Huntingdon, named for Selina Hastings, Countess of Huntingdon. Formed in 1787.
Area – 895 sq. mi. Area rank – 16th.
County Seat: Huntingdon.

INDIANA COUNTY

**Probably from the territory of Indiana. Formed in
1803. Area - 825 sq. mi. Area rank - 21st.
County Seat: Indiana.
(Indiana County is the Christmas tree capital.)**

BLAIRSVILLE - Named for John Blair of Blair's Gap, pioneer.
Founded 1792.

CLARKSBURG - Named for Clark family of pioneers. Founded
1829.

CRAMER - Named for Joseph Cramer, coal operator. Founded
1794.

GLEN CAMPBELL - Named for Charles Campbell. Founded
1889.

HOOVERHURST - Named for Nathan L. Hoover, pioneer settler.
Founded 1878.

INDIANA - Named from former prevalence of redmen. Founded
1809.

JACKSONVILLE - Named for President Andrew Jackson. Founded 1852.

McWEAVERTOWN - Founded 1946.

PINE FLATS - Named for great forest of pine trees in vicinity.
Founded 1860.

PLUMVILLE - Named from wild plum trees which formerly grew here. Founded 1816.

ROSSITER - Named for E. V. W. Rossiter noted railroad official. Founded 1860.

JEFFERSON COUNTY

**Named for Thomas Jefferson..Formed in 1804.
Area – 652 sq. mi. Area rank – 34th.
County Seat: Brookville.**

BROCKWAY - Named for Brockway family, pioneers. Founded 1822.

BROOKVILLE - Village of Springs or Brooks. Gateway to Cook Forest. Founded 1797.

CORSICA - Named after the birthplace of Napoleon Boneparte. Founded 1802.

EMERICKVILLE - Named for Emerick family. Founded 1840.

FALLS CREEK - Named for Falls Creek, famous in lumber days. Founded 1840.

PUNXSUTAWNEY - Name of Indian origin. Founded 1818.

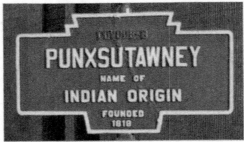

REYNOLDSVILLE - Named for Reynolds family, first settlers. Founded 1822.

SIGEL - Named for General Franz Sigel, U.S.A. Founded 1865.

JUNIATA COUNTY

**Named for the Juniata River, an Iroquois word.
Formed in 1831. Area – 386 sq. mi. Area rank – 58th.
County Seat: Mifflintown.**

McALISTERVILLE - Named for Hugh McAlister. Founded 1810.

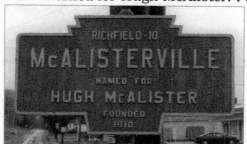

MEXICO - Formerly New Mexico, named for the Republic of
Mexico by Tobias Kreider. Founded 1810.
MIFFLINTOWN - Named for Governor Mifflin. Founded 1790.

PORT ROYAL - Formerly "Perrysville," named for Commodore
   Perry. Founded 1812.

RICHFIELD - Laid out by Christian Graybill. Founded 1818.

THOMPSONTOWN - Named for William Thompson. Founded
   1755.

LACKAWANNA COUNTY

**From the Delaware Indian name Lechauhanne. Formed
in 1878. (Last of the 67 counties to be formed.) Area –
454 sq. mi. Area rank – 49th. County Seat: Scranton.**

MONTDALE - Named for the mountains on either side. Founded
   1800.

LANCASTER COUNTY
Named for Lancashire, England. Formed in 1729.
Area – 946 sq. mi. Area rank – 12th.
County Seat: Lancaster.

ADAMSTOWN - Named for William Adams, pioneer settler. Founded 1761.

AKRON - Formerly New Berlin. Named for city in Ohio. Founded 1833.

BAINBRIDGE - Named for Commodore William Bainbridge, U. S. N. Founded 1813.

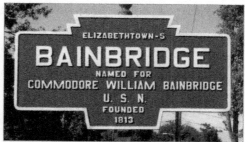

BIRD-IN-HAND - Named for a picture on old hotel's swinging sign. Founded 1734.

BLUE BALL - Named for "The Blue Ball Hotel." Founded 1766.

BRICKERVILLE - Named for Peter Bricker, pioneer settler. Founded 1741.

BRIGHTON - Established 1997.

BROWNSTOWN - Named for early settlers named Brown. Founded 1729.

CHRISTIANA - Named for pioneer settler Christiana Noble. Founded 1833.

CHURCHTOWN - Named for the prevalance of churches in early days. Founded 1740.

CLAY - Named for Henry Clay. Founded 1740.

COLUMBIA - Formerly "Wright's Ferry" renamed after Revolutionary War. Founded 1726.

CONESTOGA - Home of the Conestoga Wagon. Formerly Conestoga Centre. Founded by John Kendig 1805.

DENVER - Formerly Union Station named after Denver, Colorado by Adam G. Brubaker. Incorporated 1900.

EAST PETERSBURG - Founded by Daniel Wolf, pioneer settler. Founded 1800.*

ELIZABETHTOWN - Named for Elizabeth Hughes, early settler. Founded 1746.

EPHRATA - Biblical name. Formerly Kloster and Dunkerstown. Founded 1750.

GAP - Named for gap in hills. Founded 1701.

GOODVILLE - Named for Peter Good, early landowner and settler. Founded 1815.

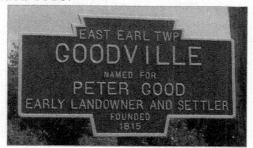

HINKLETOWN - Named for George Hinkle. Founded 1767.

INTERCOURSE - Formerly "Cross Keys," from a noted old tavern stand. Founded 1754.

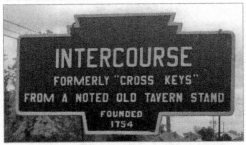

KINZER - Named for Harry Kinzer, descendant of Huguenot settlers. Founded 1835.

LANCASTER - Named for town and shire in England. Founded 1730.

LANDISVILLE - Named for John Landis. Founded 1808.

LEAMAN PLACE - Named for Henry Leaman, noted early landowner. Founded 1835.

LEXINGTON - Formerly "Dundee." Renamed for Battle of Lexington. Founded 1805.

LINCOLN - Formerly New Ephrata, renamed for President Lincoln. Founded 1814. (Now part of Ephrata borough.)

LITITZ - Founded by Count Zinzendorf, Moravian missionary. Founded 1756.

MANHEIM - Founded 1762.

MARIETTA - Named for Mary and Henrietta Anderson. Founded 1719.

MARTICVILLE - Formerly "Frogtown," named for Martic family of pioneers. Founded 1711.

MAYTOWN - So named being founded on the first day of May. Founded 1762.

MOUNT JOY - Formerly Richland. Renamed for one of William Penn's manors. Founded 1768.

MOUNTVILLE - Modification of former name, Mount Pleasant. Founded 1814.

NEFFSVILLE - Named for John Neff. Founded 1806.

NEW DANVILLE - Named for early settlers named Daniel. Founded 1780.

NEW HOLLAND - Formerly Earltown and New Design. Founded 1728.

NEW PROVIDENCE - Formerly Black Horse, from a noted old tavern stand. Founded 1730.

PARADISE - Named by Joshua Scott. Founded 1804.

QUARRYVILLE - Named for noted quarries located here. Founded 1791.

REAMSTOWN - Formerly Zoar, renamed for Tobias Ream. Founded 1760.

REFTON - Founded by Daniel Herr, pioneer. Founded 1877.

ROTHSVILLE - Named for Philip Roth, early settler and tavern keeper. Formerly Rabbit Hill. Founded 1790.

SALUNGA - Abbreviated from Indian name, Chickies Salunga Creek. Founded 1760.

SCHOENECK - "Des is en Schoenes Eck." "This is a pretty corner." Est. circa 1732.

SOUDERSBURG - Named for Jacob Souders, pioneer. Founded 1727.*

STRASBURG - Named after a cathedral city of Europe. Founded 1733.

TALMAGE - Formerly Earlville, still called Graffville. Founded 1729.

WASHINGTON BORO - Formerly Washington Village. Founded by Jacob Dritt, Esq. Founded 1807.

LAWRENCE COUNTY

Named for Perry's Flagship, which was named for Captain James Lawrence. Formed in 1850. Area – 367 sq. mi. Area rank – 60th. County Seat: New Castle.

MOUNT JACKSON - Named for General Andrew Jackson. Founded 1815.

LEBANON COUNTY

**Named for Lebanon Township, from Hebrew word Leba-
non, "white mountains." Formed in 1813. Area – 363
sq. mi. Area rank – 61st. County Seat: Lebanon.**

ANNVILLE - Formerly Millerstown, renamed for Ann Miller, wife
of the founder. Founded 1762.

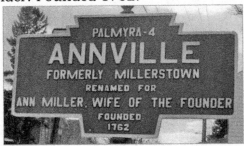

CAMPBELLTOWN - Founded by John Campbell 1759.
CLEONA - Name derived from Greek word meaning "glory." Incorporated 1929.

CORNWALL - Named for Cornwall, England. Founded 1742.

FREDERICKSBURG - Formerly Stumpstown, renamed for Frederick Stump. Founded 1761.

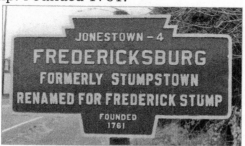

JONESTOWN - Formerly Williamsburg, renamed for founder William Jones. Founded 1761.

LICKDALE - 1884. Formerly Union Forge - 1782. Renamed for James Lick. (Present sign erected April 1991.)

MYERSTOWN - Named for Isaac Myers, founder. Founded 1768.

PALMYRA - Originally called "Palmstown," for founded John Palm. Founded 1749.

QUENTIN - Formerly named Bismarck, changed its name to Quentin in honor of President Theodore Roosevelt's son, in 1918, due to anti-German feelings.

RICHLAND - Established 1906.

LEHIGH COUNTY

From Indian name Lechauwekink, shortened to Lecha, later Anglisized as Lehigh. Formed in 1812. Area – 348 sq. mi. Ares rank – 62nd. County Seat: Allentown.

CENTER VALLEY - So named being surrounded by high hills. Founded 1745.

COOPERSBURG - Named for Judge Cooper, Colonial jurist. Founded 1780.

NEW SMITHVILLE - Named for Solomon Smith. Founded 1866.

SCHNECKSVILLE - Named for first settler, Daniel Schneck. Founded 1840.

TREXLERTOWN - Named for John Trexler, proprietor of first hotel. Founded 1760.

VERA CRUZ - Named by Alexander Weaver. Founded 1851.

WESCOSVILLE - Named for first postmaster, Israel Wesco. Founded 1809.

LUZERNE COUNTY

Named for Anne Cesar, Chevalier de la Luzerne, a brother of Cardinal de la Luzerne. Formed in 1786. Area – 886 sq. mi. Area rank – 17th. County Seat: Wilkes-Barre.

CONYNGHAM - Named for Conyngham family. Founded 1805.

EXETER - Named for Exeter in Rhode Island. Founded 1884.

FORTY FORT - From fort built by first forty settlers. Founded 1780.*

HARVEY'S LAKE - Named for Benjamin Harvey, pioneer land-owner. Founded 1775.*

MOUNTAIN TOP - So named from location on mountain top. Founded 1788.

SHAVERTOWN - Named for Phillip Shaver, early settler. Founded 1813.

TRUCKSVILLE - Named for William Trucks, early settler. Founded 1809.

WEST PITTSTON - Named for William Pitt, British statesman. Founded 1857.

WYOMING - Incorporated 1885.

LYCOMING COUNTY

Named for Lycoming Creek, Delaware Indian word meaning "sandy or gravelly creek." Formed in 1795. Area – 1216 sq. mi. Area rank – 1st. (About the size of Rhode Island.) County Seat: Williamsport.

CLARKSTOWN - Named for Clark family of early landowners. Founded 1850.*

LAIRDSVILLE - Named for John Laird, pioneer settler. Founded 1829.

MONTGOMERY - Named for real estate owner R. B. Montgomery. Founded 1870.

MONTOURSVILLE - Named for Andrew Montour, Indian guide and interpreter. Founded 1768.

MUNCY - Name derived from Monsey or Wolf Tribe Indians. Surveyed 1769.

PICTURE ROCKS - From huge Indian murals painted on rocks overlooking creek. Founded 1848.

RALSTON - Named for Matthew C. Ralston, noted landowner. Founded 1837.

RAMSEY VILLAGE - Settled by Thomas Ramsey, wagon master for George Washington's Continental Army. Circa 1790.

SALLADASBURG - Founded 1837 by Jacob P. Sallada.

SOUTH WIILLIAMSPORT - Section of Williamsport located on South side of Susquehanna River. Founded 1886.

WATERVILLE - Named for confluence of Tiadaghton and Little Pine Creek. Founded 1840.

WILLIAMSPORT - The former lumber city founded and laid out by Michael Ross. Founded 1795.

McKEAN COUNTY

Named for Thomas McKean, thrice-elected Governor of Pennsylvania. Formed in 1804. Area – 992 sq. mi. Area rank – 11th. County Seat: Smethport.

BRADFORD - Formerly Littlestown, renamed for Thomas Bradford. Founded 1827.

MERCER COUNTY

Named for General Hugh Mercer. Formed in 1800. Area – 670 sq. mi. Area rank – 33rd. County Seat: Mercer.

HERMITAGE - City of. Founded 1832.
SHEAKLEYVILLE - Named for George Sheakley. Founded 1818.

MIFFLIN COUNTY

Named for General Thomas Mifflin, a former Governor of the Keystone State. (1788-1799.) Formed in 1789. Area – 431 sq. mi. Area rank – 53rd. County Seat: Lewistown.

MONROE COUNTY

Named for James Monroe, 5th President of the United States. Formed in 1836. Area - 611 sq. mi. Area rank – 37th. County Seat: Stroudsburg.

MONTGOMERY COUNTY

Named for General Richard Montgomery. Formed in 1784. Area – 496 sq. mi. Area rank – 46th. County Seat: Norristown.

ABINGTON - Named for Abington Friends Meeting, England. Settled 1714.

AMBLER - Named for Mary Ambler, heroine of railroad accident. Founded 1857.

ARDMORE - Formerly "Athensville," renamed Ardmore in 1873. Founded 1873.

AUDUBON - Formerly Saylor's Corners, Jack's Tavern & Shannonville; name changed in 1899 to honor artist John James Audubon. Established Circa 1823.

BETHAYRES - Named for Elizabeth Ayres an early resident. Founded 1876.*

BLUE BELL - Formerly Pigeontown, renamed Blue Bell. Founded 1840.

BRIDGEPORT - Named on account of port and building of bridge. Founded 1829.

BRYN ATHYN - From the Welsh words meaning "hill" and "cohesive." Founded 1895.

BRYN MAWR - Formerly Humphreysville, renamed Bryn Mawr in 1858. Founded 1858.

CENTER SQUARE - Named for the junction of State Road and Skippack Turnpike. Founded 1727.

COLLEGEVILLE - So named due to multiple colleges being located here. Founded 1896.

EAGLEVILLE - Folklore states the name refers to an eagle tacked to a barn door by a local hunter. Established circa 1853.

EAST GREENVILLE - Named for large pine tree in northern section of town. Founded 1802.

ELKINS PARK - Originally Shoemakerstown, then Ogontz, re-named Elkins Park. Founded 1746.

FLOURTOWN - Name derived from pioneers coming to mills for flour. Settled 1743.

FORT WASHINGTON - Named for encampment of Washington's Army, October to December 1777.

GILBERTSVILLE - Named for John Bernhart Gilbert, early Huguenot settler. Founded 1785.

GRATERFORD - Named for Jacob Kreater an early settler. Founded 1756.

GREEN LANE - Named for the foliage of the trees growing along the road. Founded 1749.

HARLEYSVILLE - Named for Samuel Harley, an early Quaker settler. Founded 1776.

HATBORO - Hats were manufactured here for soldiers during the Revolutionary War. Founded 1706.

HATFIELD - Named for John Hatfield, noted pioneer settler. Founded 1734.

JARRETTOWN - Named for Levi Jarrett, an early settler. Founded 1876.

JEFFERSONVILLE - Named for Jefferson Inn. Founded 1776.

JENKINTOWN - Named after Stephen Jenkins, an early Welsh settler. Founded 1759.

KING OF PRUSSIA - Named for Frederick the Great of Prussia. Founded 1786.

KULPSVILLE - Named for Jacob Kulp, an early settler. Founded 1773.

LANSDALE - Named for Phillip Lansdale Fox chief surveyor North Penn. R. R. Co. Founded 1856.

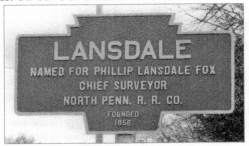

LIMERICK - Named for a city and county in Ireland. Founded 1722.

MONTGOMERYVILLE - Named for a county in North Wales. Founded 1717.

NOBLE - Named for Samuel W. Noble, early settler and land-owner. Founded 1839.

NORRISTOWN - Named for Isaac Norris, patriot. Founded 1784.

PENNSBURG - Formerly Heiligsville. Founded 1735.

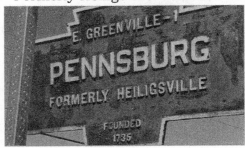

PERKIOMENVILLE - Indian name meaning "somewhat clouded." Founded 1704.*

PLYMOUTH MEETING - Named for township and meeting house. Founded 1685.

POTTSTOWN - Named for John Potts, the founder. Founded 1753.

RAHNS - Named for George Rahn, an early settler. Founded 1865.

RED HILL - Named from the color of the soil. Founded 1836.

ROYERSFORD - Named for Royer family, distinguished Huguenot settlers. Incorporated 1879. Founded 1709.

SANATOGA - From the Indian, "a crooked hill." Founded 1770.

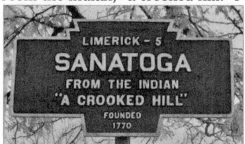

SCHWENKSVILLE - Named for George Schwenk, early settler. Founded 1756.

SKIPPACK - Indian name meaning "still waters" or "pool". Founded 1704.

SOUDERTON - Named in honor of Henry O. Souder, an early businessman. Founded 1876.

SPRING HOUSE - Name derived from stone spring house. Founded 1698.

SUMNEYTOWN - Named for Isaac Sumney, an early settler. Founded 1763.

TRAPPE - Named from the German "Treppe," meaning "steps." Founded 1745.

TROOPER - Village of. According to folklore the name came from a local inn's sign depicting a trooper. Established circa 1884.

TYLERSPORT - Named for John Tyler, President of the U. S. Founded 1728.

WILLOW GROVE - Name derived from willow trees. Founded 1711.

WYNNEWOOD - Named for Dr. Thomas Wynne, physician to William Penn and first Speaker of the First Pennsylvania Assembly. Settled 1691.

ZIEGLERSVILLE - Named for Andrew Ziegler, pioneer settler. Founded 1804.

MONTOUR COUNTY

Named for Madame Montour, famous Indian interpreter. Formed in 1850. Area – 130 sq. mi. Area rank 66th. County Seat: Danville.

DANVILLE - Named for General Daniel Montgomery, Revolutionary patriot. Founded 1792.

EXCHANGE - Named for Horse Exchange on old mail route in coaching days. Founded 1840.

MOORESBURG - Named for Moore family of pioneers. Founded 1806.

STRAWBERRY RIDGE - Named for ridge where wild strawberries grow. Founded 1890.

WASHINGTONVILLE - Named for George Washington. Founded 1815.*

WHITE HALL - Named for White Hall Hotel. Formerly Fruitstown. Founded 1800.

NORTHAMPTON COUNTY

Named for Northamptonshire, England. Formed in 1752. Area - 376 sq. mi. Area rank - 59th. County Seat: Easton.

EASTON - Named for Easton, England, home of founder. Founded 1742.

HELLERTOWN - Named after Christopher Heller, pioneer and first settler. Founded 1742.

NAZARETH - Named by George Whitefield. Founded 1740.

PORTLAND - Named after Capt. James Ginn's home, Portland, Maine. Founded 1845.

STOCKERTOWN - Named for first settler, Jonas Stocker. Founded 1774.

WILSON - Renamed for President Woodrow Wilson. Founded 1742.*

NORTHUMBERLAND COUNTY

Named for Northumberland County, England. Formed in 1772. Area 453 sq. mi. Area rank - 50th. County Seat: Sunbury.

AUGUSTAVILLE - Named for Port Augusta. of Indian War fame. Founded 1860.

DALMATIA - Formerly Georgetown, renamed for shore resemblance to Dalmatia coast of Europe. Founded 1798.

DEWART - Named for Congressman William L. Dewart. Formerly Uniontown. Founded 1857.

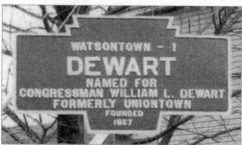

DORNSIFE - Named for Harry Dornsife, pioneer and landowner. Founded 1878.

ELYSBURG - Named for Ely family. Formerly Petersburg. Founded 1830.

HERNDON - Named for Commodore Herndon, U. S. N. Founded 1854.

KULPMONT - Named for Honorable Monroe H. Kulp, congressman and landowner.*

McEWENSVILLE - Formerly "Pine Grove," renamed for Alex McEwen. Founded 1790.

MANDATA - Named for Indian girl who lived where the town is now located. Founded 1880.

MILTON - Meaning "Milltown," from mill built on Limestone Run. Founded 1768.*

MONTANDON - Named for Peter Montandon, famous Huguenot leader. Formerly Cameronia. Founded 1825.

NORTHUMBERLAND - From the English town and county - Northumberland. Founded 1772.

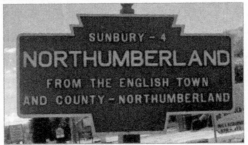

PAXINOS - Named for Swanee Indian chief. Founded 1769.

POTTSGROVE - Named for Hans Potts, early pioneer settler. Founded 1821.

SHAMOKIN - From the Indan, "The place of the horns." Founded 1773.

SUNBURY - Formerly "Shamokin." Renamed after Sunbury, England. Founded 1770.

TURBOTVILLE - Formerly "Snydertown." Renamed for Turbot Township. Founded 1859.

UNIONTOWN - Northumberland County, Railroad Station. Tharptown, Post Office Gosstown. Founded as Uniontown in 1811.

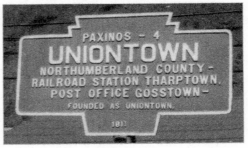

WATSONTOWN - Named by John Watson. Founded 1769.

PERRY COUNTY

Named for Commodore Oliver Hazard Perry. Formed in 1820. Area – 551 sq. mi. Area rank – 41st. County Seat: New Bloomfield.

BLAIN - Named for James Blain. Founded 1778.

DUNCANNON - Formerly Petersburg, renamed for Duncan family. Founded 1844.

ICKESBURG - Named for Nicholas Ickes. Founded 1818.

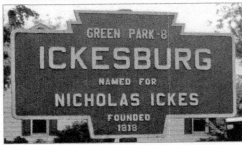

LANDISBURG - Named for Abram Landis. Founded 1793.

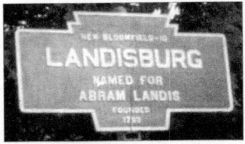

LIVERPOOL - Named for Liverpool, England. Founded 1818.

LOYSVILLE - Named for Michale Loy. Founded 1830.

MARYSVILLE - Named after railroad station. Founded 1870.

MILLERSTOWN - Named for David Miller, pioneer settler. Founded 1790.

NEW BLOOMFIELD - Named for one of the early Penn Manors. Founded 1823.

NEW BUFFALO - Named for Bison which formerly crossed river near here. Founded 1823.

NEW GERMANTOWN - Named for Germantown near Philadelphia. Founded 1820.

PHILADELPHIA COUNTY

Named for the County Seat, Philadelphia, which was named from the Biblical city in Asia Minor. Formed in 1682. Area – 129 sq. mi. Area rank – 67th. Population rank – 1st. (One of the 3 original counties. "THE CITY OF BROTHERLY LOVE."

PHILADELPHIA - Named by William Penn, from Greek word "Brotherly Love." Founded 1682.

PIKE COUNTY

Named for General Zebulon Montgomery Pike. (He discovered the mountain in Colorado that bears his name, Pike's Peak.) Formed in 1814. Area – 542 sq. mi. Area rank – 42nd. County Seat: Milford.

BUSHKILL - From the Dutch, "Little river." Founded 1815.

DELAWARE RIVER - Called Lennape Wihittuck by Native Lenni Lennape Indians. Lamasepose or Great Fishkill by early Dutch settlers. Erected 1967.

DINGMAN'S FERRY - Originally named Dingmans Choice. Founded 1735.

MATAMORAS - Named in 1848 for a town in Mexico. Upper streets laid out by J. Biddis, a Quaker, to resemble those of his native Philadelphia.

MILFORD - Named for old town in Wales. Formerly called Wells Ferry. Founded 1767.

SHOHOLA - Named for Shohola Creek, an Indian tribe. Founded 1772.

POTTER COUNTY

Named for General James Potter. Formed in 1804.
Area – 1092 sq. mi. Area rank – 6th.
County Seat: Coudersport. "GOD'S COUNTRY."

AUSTIN - Founded 1856 on land owned by E. O. Austin. Incorporated September 21, 1888.

GENESEE - Named for Genesee River. Founded 1825.

GOLD - So named due to early prosperity of village. Founded 1857.

SWEDEN VALLEY - Named by early settlers from Sweden. Founded 1807.

SCHUYLKILL COUNTY

**Named for Schuylkill River. Formed in 1811. Area –
784 sq. mi. Area rank – 26th. County Seat: Pottsville.**

BRANCH DALE - Once known as Muddy Creek. Founded 1836.

CRESSONA - Established 1857.

DONALDSON - Named for William Donaldson, coal operator. Founded 1837.

FOUNTAIN SPRINGS - Laid out by Nicholas Seitzinger, pioneer settler. Founded 1795.

FRACKVILLE - Founded 1876.

GOWEN CITY - Named for Franklin Gowen, capitalist and landowner. Founded 1885.

HEGINS - Named for Judge Hegins.

MIDDLEPORT - From location midway between Pottsville and Tamaqua. Founded 1821.

MINERSVILLE - Name derived from mining industry. Founded 1830.

PINE GROVE - First settlement surrounded by grove of pines. Founded 1830.

PORT CARBON - From large shipments of coal by water. Founded 1811.

SUEDBURG - Formerly Mifflin, named for town in Sweden. Founded 1873.

TAMAQUA - From the Indian, "Running water." Founded 1829.

TREMONT - Established 1816.

VALLEY VIEW - Named from its visibility from any point in valley. Founded 1874.

SNYDER COUNTY

Named for Simon Snyder. Formed in 1855. Area – 327 sq. mi. Area rank – 63rd. County Seat: Middleburg.

BEAVER SPRINGS - Originally Reigertown, renamed by P. O. Dept. Founded 1806.

FREEBURG - Originally called Straubstown for founder Andrew Straub. Founded 1796.

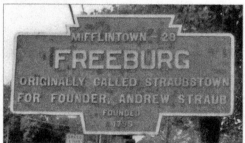

KRATZERVILLE - Formerly "Hessler's" renamed for Daniel Kratzer. Founded 1847.

KREAMER - Originally called Smiths Grove. Founded 1781.
McCLURE - Named for Alex. McClure. Founded 1867.

MIDDLEBURG - Originally "Swinefordstown, " renamed for Middleburg, Holland. Founded 1765.*

PAXTONVILLE - Formerly "Kearn's Mills," renamed for Robert Paxton. Founded 1882.

PORT TREVORTON - Named for John B. Trevor, New York. Founded 1853.

SALEM - Named for New Salem Church. Founded 1813.

SELINSGROVE - Named for the founder, Major Anthony Selin. Founded 1755. Selinsgrove home of Susquehanna University, a Christian college for men and women. Founded 1858. *

TROXELVILLE - Named for John Troxel. Founded 1856.

SOMERSET COUNTY

Named for Somerset County, England. Formed in 1795. Area – 1078 sq. mi. Area rank – 7th. County Seat: Somerset. (Highest County Seat in State with an elevation of 2,200 ft.)

ADDISON - Formerly Petersburg, renamed for Judge Addison. Founded 1789.

BAKERSVILLE - Named for founder Henry Baker. Founded 1847.

CONFLUENCE - Named from location at junction of three streams. Founded 1878.

DAVIDSVILLE - Named for founder, David Stutzman. Founded 1831.

HARNEDSVILLE - Named for founder Samuel Harned. Founded 1836.

HOLSOPPLE - Named for founder Charles Holsopple. Founded 1880.

HOOVERSVILLE - Named for founder Jonas Hoover. Founded 1836.

JENNERSTOWN - Named for Dr. Edward Jenner, originator of vaccination. Founded 1822.

LAVANSVILLE - Named for founder David Lavan.

NEW CENTREVILLE - So named, due to location between Gephartsburg and New Lexington. Founded 1834.

SHANKSVILLE - Named for early settler Christian Shank. Founded 1803.

SULLIVAN COUNTY

Named for General John Sullivan. Formed in 1847.
Area – 478 sq. mi. Area rank – 48th.
County Seat: Laporte.

EAGLES MERE - Originally Lewis Lake, renamed from "Lake of the Eagles." Founded 1804.

FORKSVILLE - Named from location at forks of Big and Little Loyalsock Creeks. Founded 1810.

LAPORTE - Named for John Laporte, Surveyor General of Penna. Founded 1847.

MILDRED - Named for Mildred McDonald. Founded 1870.

MUNCY VALLEY - Named from Valley of Muncy Creek. Founded 1867.

WRIGHT'S VIEW - Named in honor of former Secretary of Highways P. D. Wright.

SUSQUEHANNA COUNTY

Named for the Susquehanna River, because it enters Pennsylvania in this county. Formed in 1810. Area – 833 sq. mi. Area rank – 20th. County Seat: Montrose.

FOREST CITY - So named being settled in heavy forests. Founded 1864.

TIOGA COUNTY

Named for the Tioga River. Formed in 1804. Area – 1146 sq. mi. Area rank – 3rd. County Seat: Wellsboro.

ANSONIA - Named for Anson Phelps, wealthy lumberman.
AUSTINBURG - Named for William Austin, pioneer settler. Founded 1835.

BLOSSBURG - Peters Camp now Blossburg. Coal discovered 1792 by Patterson Brothers noted Indian scouts. (Edge of town.)

Named for Aaron Bloss, first settler. Founded 1802. (Center of town.)

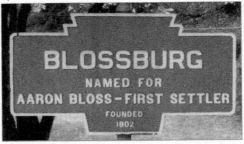

COVINGTON - Named for city in Kentucky. Founded 1801.

COWANESQUE - Named for an Indian chief. Founded 1858.

GAINES - Named for Richard Pendelton Gaines, early settler. Founded 1805.

KEENEYVILLE - Named for Elias Keeney, pioneer settler. Founded 1835.

LAWRENCEVILLE - Named for Commodore James Lawrence, U. S. N. Founded 1787.

MAINESBURG - Named for John Maine, pioneer settler.

MIDDLEBURY - Named for location midway between Tioga and Wellsboro. Founded 1824.

MORRIS - Named for Benjamin Wistar Morris, landowner and Capitalist of Philadelphia. Founded 1799.

ROARING BRANCH - Named for stream of the same name. Founded 1862.

SHORTSVILLE - Named for Short family of pioneers. Founded 1840.

TIOGA - Named after Tioga River, Indian word meaning "our gateway." Founded 1792.

WELLSBORO - Named for Mary Wells, wife of Benjamin Morris, landowner. Founded 1800.

WESTFIELD - So named, being western limit of Cowansque Valley. Founded 1816.

UNION COUNTY

Expressing unity, "the sentiment which actuates the American people." Formed in 1813. (Almost renamed Buffalo County in 1855.) Area – 318 sq. mi. Area rank – 64th. County Seat: Lewisburg.

ALLENWOOD - Formerly Uniontown, renamed in 1871 for H. P. Allen. Settled 1815.

HARTLETON - Named for Colonel Hartley, who owned the land at time town was laid out. Founded 1793.

LAURELTON - Named for Laurel Run. Founded 1811.

LEWISBURG - Originally called Derrstown. Renamed when Snyder Co. was separated from Union Co. in 1855. Founded 1770.

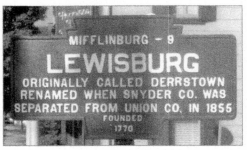

MIFFLINBURG - Named for Governor Mifflin. Founded 1792.

NEW BERLIN - Originally known as Longstown. Founded 1768.

NEW COLUMBIA - Formerly New Columbus. Founded 1818.

VICKSBURG - Named for Grant's victory at Vicksburg, Mississippi. Founded 1865.

WEST MILTON - Formerly "Datesmans" renamed West Milton from Milton. Founded 1769.

VENANGO COUNTY

Named for Venango River, now French Creek. Formed in 1800. Area – 678 sq. mi. Area rank – 32nd. County Seat: Franklin. "THE OIL COUNTY."

OIL CITY - Named for Oil Creek. Founded 1803.

WARREN COUNTY

Named for General Joseph Warren, Revolutionary patriot. Formed in 1800. Area – 905 sq. mi. Area rank – 14th. County Seat: Warren.

IRVINE - Named for General William Irvine. Founded 1820.*

PITTSFIELD - Named for Pittsfield, Mass., home of first settlers. Founded 1820.
SHEFFIELD - Named for Sheffield, England. Founded 1836.
TIDIOTE - From the Indian "Far outlook of view."
WARREN - Named in honor of General Joseph Warren. Founded 1795.

WASHINGTON COUNTY

**Named for George Washington, 1st President of U. S. A.
Formed in 1781. Area – 857 sq. mi. Area rank – 19th.
County Seat: Washington.**

AMITY - Meaning "friendly relationship." Founded 1798.
BEALLSVILLE - Named for Zephaniah Beall in 1819.

BENTLEYVILLE - Named for Sheshbazaar Bently. Founded 1816.

BUFFALO - Named for Buffalo Church. Founded 1779.

BURGETTSTOWN - Named for Sebastian Burgett. Founded
 1785.

CALIFORNIA - Historically famous as meeting place of settlers
 and Indians in 1767. Founded 1769.

CENTERVILLE - Central stopping point between Washington
 and Uniontown for stage coaches. Founded 1821.

CLAYSVILLE - Named for Henry Clay, statesman. Founded
 1781.

ELLSWORTH - Named for James W. Ellsworth. Founded 1900.

HICKORY - Originally "Hickory Tavern." Founded 1797.

INDEPENDENCE - Originally Williamsburg. Founded 1803.

NEW EAGLE - Named for the American eagle. Founded 1881.
PANCAKE - Named for George Pancake, pioneer settler. Founded 1822.

SCENERY HILL - Originally Hillsborough. Founded 1785.

WASHINGTON - Named for General George Washington. Founded 1782.

WEST MIDDLETOWN - Formerly West Middle Borough. Founded 1795.

WAYNE COUNTY

Named for General "Mad" Anthony Wayne. Formed in 1796. Area – 741 sq. mi. Area rank – 29th. County Seat: Honesdale.

GOULDSBORO - Named for Jay Gould, railroad magnate. Founded 1871.

HAWLEY - Named for Irad Hawley. Founded 1827.

WHITE MILLS - Named from old whitewashed sawmills. Founded 1865.

WESTMORELAND COUNTY

Named for Westmoreland County, England. Formed in 1773. Area – 1024 sq. mi. Area rank – 8th. County Seat: Greensburg. The last county created before the Revolution, was the first county located entirely west of the Allegheny Mountains in Pennsylvania.

ADAMSBURG - Named for John Quincy Adams. Founded 1824.
ARNOLD - Named for Andrew Arnold, pioneer settler. Founded 1852.

DELMONT - Meaning a valley in the hills. Founded 1814.

EXPORT - Named for the first export coal mined in this territory. Founded 1912.

GREENSBURG - Named for General Nathanael Green, patriot. Founded 1785.*

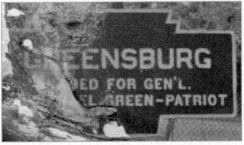

JONES MILLS - Named for Thomas Jones, pioneer settler.

LAUGHLINTOWN - Named for pioneer settler, Robert Laughlin. Founded 1797.

LIGONIER - Named by General John Forbes after Marshel Ligonier. Founded 1817.

NEW ALEXANDRIA - Named for older town of Alexandria on Juniata River. Founded 1832.

NEWLONSBURG - Named for William Newlon, pioneer settler. Founded 1822.

RUFFSDALE - Named for Ruff, pioneer settler.

TRAFFORD - Named by George Westinghouse for Trafford Park, England. Founded 1904.

YOUNGSTOWN - Named for Young family of pioneers. Founded 1800.

YOUNGWOOD - Named for Young family of pioneers. Founded
  1899.

WYOMING COUNTY

**Named for Wyoming Valley in County. Formed in
1842. Area – 398 sq. mi. Area rank – 57th.
County Seat: Tunkhannock.**

FACTORYVILLE - Incorporated 1787.
FORKSTON - Named by Ezra White for forks of stream. Founded 1830.

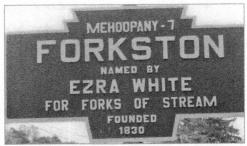

YORK COUNTY

Named for James Stuart, Duke of York, King James II; or County of York. Formed in 1749. Area – 909 sq. mi. Area rank – 13th. County Seat: York.

AIRVILLE - Named for pure air in neighborhood. Founded 1828.

CLY - Named for Clymer Shelly, an early merchant.

CRALEY - Named for George Craley, pioneer settler. Founded 1845.

DALLASTOWN - Named for Vice President George M. Dallas. Founded 1736.

DILLSBURG - Named for first settler, Matthew Dill. Founded 1800. (This sign was originally used at borough boundry lines to display town's name. Placed here by Dillsburg Lions Club to commemorate 50th Anniversary. 1931–1981.)

DOVER - Named for Dover, England. Founded 1752.

EAST PROSPECT - Named from fine view of the surrounding country. Founded 1735.

FARMERS - Established 1830.

FRANKLINTOWN - Named for Benjamin Franklin. Founded 1813.

GLEN ROCK - Originally Rocks in Glen. Founded 1838.

GOLDSBORO - Named for Major Goldsboro, distinguished civil engineer. Founded 1850.

HALLAM - Named for Hallam, England. Founded 1850.
HANOVER - Named for Hanover, Germany. Founded 1745.

JACOBUS - Named for Jacob Geiselman. Founded 1837.

JEFFERSON - Post Office, Codorus, PA. Named for Thomas Jefferson. Founded 1812.

LEWISBERRY - Named for Eli Lewis. Founded 1734.

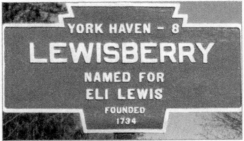

LOGANVILLE - Named for Colonel Henry Logan. Founded 1820.

MANCHESTER - Named for Manchester, England. Founded 1740.

MT. WOLF - Named for George Wolf, Governor of Pennsylvania 1830–1836. Founded 1850.

RED LION - Named from a nearby tavern stand. Founded 1736.

SEVEN VALLEYS - Named for the siebenthal or "seven valleys" within view of borough. Founded 1892.

SPRING GROVE - Named for spring surrounded by large groves. Founded 1747.

STEWARTSTOWN - Named for one of first settlers, Anthony Stewart. Founded 1767.

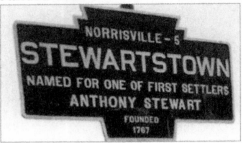

STRINESTOWN - Originally "Mt. Pleasant," renamed for John Strine. Founded 1800.*

THOMASVILLE - Named for first postmaster, George B. Thomas. Founded 1870.

WELLSVILLE - Named for Abraham Wells. Founded 1737.

WINDSOR - Formerly Windsorville, named for Windsor, England. Founded 1905.

WRIGHTSVILLE - Named for first settler, John Wright. Founded 1732.

YORK HAVEN - So named being a haven for transportation down Susquehanna River. Founded 1814.

YORK NEW SALEM - Named by settlers from York County and for Salem, Massachusetts. Founded 1876.

ZION VIEW - Named in 1890 after Zions Church. Founded 1757.

OTHER PENNSYLVANIA LANDMARKS
Creeks, Rivers, and Streams

Allegheny River (Near Parker)

Antes Creek (Near Jersey Shore)

Beech Creek Stream (Near Monument)

Bermudian Creek (Idaville)*

Buffalo Creek (New Buffalo)

Conewago Creek (Biglerville)

Crum Creek (Norwood)

Dunnings Creek

Glade Run

Hay Creek (Birdsboro)

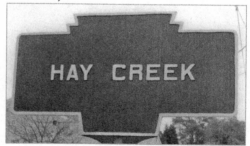

Little Muncy Creek

Mahantango Creek*

Mehoopany Creek (Forkston)

Middle Creek

Mill Creek

Penn's Creek (New Berlin & Mifflinburg)

Ramsey Run (Waterville)

Rock Creek (Adams County)

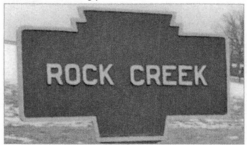

Youghiogheny River (Versailles)

OTHER PENNSYLVANIA LANDMARKS
MISCELLANEOUS

1924 Pennsylvania State Highway

1934 Pennsylvania Highway

Angora Bridge

Cornwall Borough Line

Dickinson College

Greenwood Nursery

Mt. Pleasant Street

Pontius Cemetery

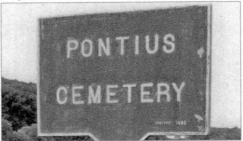

School Zone

Shippensburg University

Tresspass Notice

About the Author

N.(orman) Clair Clawser has had many interests since graduating from Hershey High School in 1963. He took Print Shop for three years in high school. He has been interested in Geography and his home state. This contributes to the compilation of signs. Interested in books and making them from very early in life, he has done various other small publications including quite a bit of cartooning. Has been published in "Pennsylvania Magazine" and "Lancaster Magazine" plus "Apprise" and "Susquehanna Life."*

Clair has written many poems on various subjects. He is an avid runner having completed 1,138 runs since 1979.

* Had a brief run with a cartoon
strip "Little Suzie Sunbream" in the
Lititz Record Express in 2005.

(Answer to question on page vii: Ben Franklin spelled backwards)

CPSIA information can be obtained
at www.ICGtesting.com
Printed in the USA
BVOW08*0056151216
469709BV00011B/10/P

9 781620 067376